BE THE BEST

Honest practical lessons from successes and failures in building businesses and teams.

Let's aim to be thinking always about changing and improving. If we can only change just one small thing we do each week, in a year we can radically change our own lives and the lives of others. Even just one thing a month will be significant over time.

Paperback copies available through Lulu, Amazon and Createspace.

Electronic copies available on Kindle (Amazon).

ISBN: 978-1-48483-864-8

Copyright © Mark Richard Bates 2013.

Fourth edition 2015.

The moral right of the author has been asserted.

All rights reserved.

Without limiting the rights under copyright reserved above, no part of this publication may be reproduced, stored in or introduced into a retrieval system, or transmitted, in any form or by any means (electronic, mechanical, photocopying, recording or otherwise), without the prior written permission of the copyright owner.

About the Author

The author has spent over 25 years working as a director and manager in both private equity backed and public companies, across a wide variety of sectors.

The insight for this book comes from leading and working with some remarkable people in several business turn-rounds. The emphasis there was on practical and dynamic business change through the development of great management teams and a new staff culture that was motivated by and engaged in the challenge and rewards from working together to create a truly great business.

Underpinning this has been a focus on trying to build businesses which are unique and mould breakers in their sectors, and more engaged with staff and customers than the competition.

A particular recent emphasis has been to succeed through achieving a deep understanding of Customer Experience, creating committed "recommender" relationships with customers, and knowing how staff and company culture can influence this hugely.

The author's view is that leading a business and being a truly professional manager is one of the highest callings anyone can aspire to. Anyone with the title of "manager" ought to be proud of it, and aim to act with pride in the job at all times.

Dedication

To my wife, Fiona, and our daughters – Phoebe, Olivia and Isobel – who knew nothing about any of what went on at work, and would have been rather worried if they had known. They made sure all of the other important things were taken care of!

Preface

Any resemblance to real events or people in this book is unsurprising; it all happened. But you'll have a tough time identifying people unless, of course, it's you……and you all know who you are. I owe you all a debt of gratitude for what we went through and learned together. You were all brilliant, and <u>you are the people who really wrote this book, not me</u>.

I've been very fortunate in my career; through all of the successes and failures, one theme has been constant – the opportunity to make a real difference (for good or ill) to a lot of people, even though often I couldn't see it. Over 30 years, I've had the chance to work with some very fine managers and people at all levels, and across every functional area, and to achieve business success (as well as failure).

There have been some great successes and amazing managers, developed often from unlikely people. I've also let people down, making mistakes in learning to be a better manager; some things I've said and done make me cringe today. So, if you're one who suffered from my inadequacies, this is my apology. Don't call me to say I don't live up to the book's standards – I already know that! But my personal failures don't make the standards any less worth pursuing; we should all try our best to set an example to be proud of, and for future managers to aspire to. The only real way to fail is in not giving it your very best shot.

The book distils some key lessons on business and management (applicable to both B2B and B2C businesses) into simple, practical thinking and ideas for managers and leaders. Then offers them to you in an informal conversational style – as if we were chatting over coffee. The book aims to reach a wider audience with these ideas; to try to "do some good."

Rather than long chapters or a systematic management methodology, there's a series of nuggets on a wide variety of subjects, in order to stimulate your own thinking – written from the point of view of a manager and leader. It's a short book that aims to open up important areas in business and to generate in you some very long thought processes and action programs. There are layers of meaning in each subject, but you have to discover them for yourself, since the purpose of the book is to help you to change and improve, which only you can do.

The book is meant to be used in different ways; it could be the start of a personal program, you could read relevant chapters at need, or glance at it when you wish. You could carry it round, or leave it on your desk for others to dip into, or pass it on. I suggest you first read it all slowly and then decide for yourself, remembering that it's meant not just to be read but used; your copy is meant to end up dog-eared and covered in your own notes!

Therefore promise me one thing: that you won't leave it in a drawer or cupboard to rot, where it can do no good – which is where most of these books end up. The book is aimed at people whose mind-set is to Be the Best they can be, and it needs to be read <u>and used regularly</u>. If you don't want the book anymore, give it to some-one else who it might help. Or, if you like the book and know of managers and leaders who might find it useful, then please recommend it or get them a copy, to help them improve. And if you have some feedback for me on how to make the book better, then put a review on Amazon or write to me at mark@bethebestbusiness.co

Remember, my reason for writing the book is to try to "do some good" and, if I've got it right, <u>you can be my partner</u> in helping to spread the goodness around.

Whatever you do, I urge you to see these simple practical chapters as just the starting point to provoke some deep thinking within yourself, and action plans to change. You see, I can't actually tell you how to be a better leader and manager - only you can find that out for yourself - and you will need to think hard, and act and learn from everything in here, as well as from your own story so far, if you are going to achieve all of the potential you already have inside of you.

Putting it bluntly, you shouldn't even waste your time reading this book unless you are going to put into action anything you learn. Too many management books are read and provoke a strong positive reaction in the reader, but nothing then changes.

So, I hope you find the book to be of genuine practical use as you enjoy one of the greatest adventures of all - managing a team and building a business that wants to Be the Best.

Mark Bates

Chapters

1) Reputation is everything in Business
2) B2C customers are also talking about you!
3) What to do with Recommenders
4) Ignore the consultants! Customer Experience is not that hard
5) You won't make your Customers feel Great unless your Staff feel Great
6) Get out of that office, and boot your team out as well
7) Screw-ups aren't welcome or enjoyable but……
8) The importance of Thinking; use your brain!
9) You have to become Different, Special, Unique – and that may involve breaking the rules in your sector.
10) Authenticity; you need to be yourself, but more perfectly
11) There is no universal style of successful leadership
12) Strategy nonsense; you need a simple vision
13) What might a simple strategy look like
14) Strategy; the power of the many
15) The whole team must join in
16) Give away the credit for everything
17) While you're at it, give away power as well
18) Gloat over the positive feedback you receive (after the section on giving away the credit)
19) You get more out of people by being positive with them
20) Be kinder to other points of view

21) There's no point in not trying to Be the Best that you can be
22) Do _more_ than the customers expect
23) Customers only really trust suppliers who are genuinely unselfish
24) Living up to your brand
25) Large scale change is often the result of a series of smaller changes
26) Most management truth is simple, but you need to think deeply, slowly and long about it, and spend time putting it into action.
27) If people are never going to be good enough, sort them out as soon as possible
28) Sometimes people are just in the wrong job, or have never been properly managed or given a chance
29) The most unpromising materials can sometimes be moulded
30) Desire is everything
31) Hard work
32) You have to know your people as people
33) Great managers lose their people
34) Systems are there to serve the customers and the staff, not the reverse
35) The real owners of the business are the customers, closely followed by the staff
36) Mentors and Coaches
37) What is Success?
38) Defeat and failure
39) Guard your Integrity
40) When your leadership is questioned

41) Customer satisfaction surveys (CSAT) – what goes wrong
42) Good questions to ask customers……….the 2 questions
43) Understand your customers – you need to "get" their business and them
44) Be your own customer
45) Who are the customers?
46) All you have to do is to get them to "rub along" together
47) The importance of leaders setting an example
48) Learning - what did you learn today?
49) Good people are all around you
50) Take your team away (and what to do)
51) Getting time alone; sharpening your axe; investing in yourself
52) Everyone in your business or team can have a huge influence on success
53) Importance of Persistence/Enduring - how
54) Climbing a mountain
55) Numbers/forecasting and action
56) Listening
57) Courage/bravery
58) Waiting/Patience
59) Blame is pointless (so don't point!)
60) Saying sorry – showing vulnerability
61) Loneliness – you are on your own
62) Pride
63) Just do it!

Afterword

1) Reputation is everything in Business

It took me a long time to really understand that Reputation is fundamental to business success.

A related point is that I used to believe that highly paid sales teams were the best way to expand revenues in a business, but no longer. Reputation (and recommendation) is the best driver of long-term reliable consistent growth.

The turning point was hearing that a major blue chip customer had recommended us to a new customer who'd just started with us. So, I rang up our contact to thank them for recommending us. "Nick," I said, "I just want to thank you for recommending us to XXXX plc. It's great when customers stick their necks out on our behalf and I really want to thank you for this." Nick said "Do you know, Mark, I don't remember XXXX; I recommend you all the time."

At that moment, a light went on in my head and I understood; B2B buyers, in most markets, are all viral. They all talk to each other or have other ways to find out each other's' views. In many industries, most of them have worked for the same 2 or 3 companies in their careers, so have great existing networks with other buyers and former colleagues.

Why do they talk to each other? Because most B2B purchases require a degree of trust, and that trust is lacking if you are a new supplier. So, one of the most important things that they can do is to call another of your customers who they do trust and ask their opinion (usually without you knowing!).

It takes time to build trust and a great reputation but, without it, there can be no long-term consistently great business.

Conversely, it can take an instant to lose your reputation. So, I can forgive people who make mistakes (that's part of learning and to be encouraged). But I would never tolerate anyone who deliberately or thoughtlessly puts mine or the business' reputation at risk – neither should you. People like that must be dealt with (preferably sent off to work for the competition, where they can do you some good!).

And when you lose reputation, it takes a long time to get it back. Imagine, as we were once, being at a smart reception with senior clients and being approached by a competitor who, when hearing our name, said "Aren't you the company who puts non-performing staff in the rubbish skip in the car park?"

A "story" that was 8 years old (before my time), but still remembered and influencing people.

2) B2C customers are also talking about you!

(Reputation is even more important in today's connected world)

I wrote in the last chapter about B2B buyers, but the impact of reputation on B2C buyers (consumers) has become even more important in the last few years.

It was always true, if you let down or delighted a consumer, that their friends and acquaintances were then likely to hear about your service. In todays' connected world, that positive or negative impact is magnified potentially thousands of times.

In fact, customers now have many different ways to express their feelings about you and your business; they are everywhere - they tweet, they call, they talk, they post pictures, they're in your face, they demand, they score you, they complain, they praise, they recommend, they rant and rage......you name it, they do it! The customers have never been so close before - you can almost feel them breathing down your neck, and they are. They are everywhere!

So, whether people feel positive or negative about your service, they now have an enormous platform from which to yell about it; and ignoring them isn't going to fix the problem, it will make it worse. What's more, it really doesn't matter whether they are right or wrong – they are the real owners of the business and the most important people you know. If they think they are right, that's enough for them, and any attempt to gag them or bluff them is likely only to backfire.

United Airlines found this out when they broke Dave Carroll's guitar and then refused to compensate him. His comedy song "United breaks guitars" went viral across the internet, with millions of hits on YouTube, and showed the company in a very poor light, costing them far more than his guitar would have, until they gave in and did what they should have done in the first place – replace the guitar!

So many companies are now afraid of their customers and their power – but that's the wrong approach; you need to respect customers, not fear them, as their power can work massively in your favour if you get it right for them. There's now a big platform out there for people to recommend you, and to encourage other people to try you out.

What's more, most of your competitors will not be getting this right, so it's a great opportunity to be different.

3) What to do with Recommenders

There's a fair bit in this book about the importance of Reputation and Customer Experience and how that can mobilise the most powerful sales force you will ever have – delighted customers.

But many businesses seem to have little idea of what do with their recommenders.

Imagine this actual discussion within a senior client management team:

- The question was asked if we had identified the recommenders in our key accounts and who they might be; a list was created.
- It was then asked whether these people had recommended us and how we knew that. The answer was "of course, they recommend us" but no evidence of that was provided.
- The next question was "have we asked these delighted clients to recommend us, and how?" The answer: silence

I'm not talking here about the production of dull case studies that take ages to get signed off; I'm simply talking about informally asking clients to recommend us to some other people like them.

Yet, it feels as though people would rather do cold calling than actually ask for a recommendation from a friendly client. Sometimes, it appears that people don't know how to do this in the right way, or they fear it might offend and damage a good relationship.

So, here's a possible answer. At the end of a good meeting with the client, why not try this: "Jim, you've always been a good client to us – commercial but also very fair. We value our business with you and we're always trying to find other people like you to do business with. Do you know of anyone, like yourself, who might like the service we try to provide? Just a couple of contact details and permission to use your name as a reference would be really appreciated."

This script has number of advantages: it's personal and informal; it asks for a couple of names not the client's entire contact list; it positively references your experience with the client.

So, try this out or something similar that works better for you, but don't be one of those businesses with many recommenders who are never asked to recommend.

That's like owning a car but never driving it!

4) Ignore the consultants! Customer Experience is not that hard (but you need to want to do it badly enough)

The whole idea of Customer Experience is the subject of books, seminars and consultants, and an entire industry has grown up around it….but, actually, it's a lot more straightforward than people think.

It's simply about "making every Customer feel Great" and that requires nothing more than you and every one of your people wanting to do this all the time. You need to understand that the reputation of your business or team is in the hands of each individual, and they all need to care genuinely and deeply about each customer and the experience they have of your business.

Creating great Customer Experience is often really straightforward stuff that everyone in your business can be a part of; once I was interviewing our largest customer and she surprised me by saying that we were the best supplier they had for Customer Experience. When I asked what we did that impressed her, she said "you always answer the phone straight away, it never goes to voice-mail; nothing is too much trouble; decisions never need to be escalated up, your staff take the decisions there and then; you're always chirpy and cheerful, even when I know you're having a tough day; you always remember the personal touches, like my birthday and when I've been on holiday". All things that other big blue chip suppliers were not doing for her – we were different

The personal touches (personalisation) in Customer Experience are such an important element. Once I was having a discussion with a client about their high churn rates. At a point in our debate, the client said to me "well, at least we've got 5 million customers". That was the issue – the Customer Experience made customers feel as though they were just one in 5 million, a tiny unimportant molecule swept along in the company's giant faceless processes. So, when renewal time came, there was no loyalty. Personalising the experience, making it look at least a little bespoke, finding ways to make customers feel that they are <u>individually</u> important – all of these things will bind customers to us.

There's no big secret in this – much of it is just basic good manners and finding new ways to make customers feel valued, appreciated and special.

Not only that, it doesn't have to cost a lot of money to "make every Customer feel Great" – which is the reason many businesses shy away from going down this path.

And there's also nothing hard or complicated here. It's usually the simple things that "make every Customer feel Great"; and, because it's so simple, everyone in the business can actually understand it and get on board – there should be no exceptions allowed in your staff.

So, amazing Customer Experience can be delivered - you just need to want to deliver it badly and for everyone to take responsibility, behind a simple theme – like "Let's make every Customer feel Great".

What stops businesses doing this is usually that, deep down, behind all of the slick presentations, the staff don't actually believe that Customer Experience is one of their biggest priorities and the key to future success. They have other pressing priorities – like sweating the maximum profit out of customers, or internal politics, or meetings to go to etc.

In reality, these businesses just don't want to deliver great Customer Experience badly enough.

Ask yourself whether your business is really like this, and act to change.

5) You won't make your Customers feel Great unless your Staff feel Great

You'd think that this was obvious wouldn't you?

Yet we all go into businesses regularly where there are staff who look disengaged, bored or miserable; you either have to remove people who are like this or turn them around; and that depends largely on your personal leadership.

You won't do that by staying in your office – you have to be out in the business with the people on the front line – every day, if possible - talking to them face to face about the strategy and vision of the business. Not just talking to them, but also listening to their ideas and concerns about the business, and acting on their feedback. Only by listening and acting, can you show people that they really do matter - and can play a key part in the business, and thereby get much more out of their jobs.

Articulating a simple but compelling vision for the business, getting that across effectively to the staff, and making them feel great to be a part of it – is right at the core of what leaders have to do to get staff on board and make them as enthusiastic about the business as you are.

If the staff aren't happy and positive, that's one of the most damaging things possible for your business, as they engage with your customers every day, or engage with people who do talk to your customers. The misery always spreads and leadership is required to stop it and turn it around.

Unsurprisingly, the reverse effect occurs when you get this right and the staff are positive with customers all the time. The customers respond with appreciation, and the staff feel great about themselves and even more motivated to look after the customers. Then your business really starts to fly.

But the starting point is that your staff must feel great about being in your business.

6) Get out of that office, and boot your team out as well

(Spend as much time as possible with your customers and with your people)

Sticking to the office theme, how much of the time are you really out there on the front-line with the customers and the staff, where you'll learn best what is really going on in the business.

No, answer that question honestly; I don't believe the first answer that you gave!

You see the reality is that most of us spend far too much time every day on things that are lower priorities – set-piece meetings, answering e-mails, writing reports, being "in the office". And we all have the ready-made excuses and reasons as to why this is important.

The real reasons why we spend so much time on stuff that may not matter very much is less attractive than the reasons we give: it's a comfort-blanket or the office itself is a good place to hide; or we'd prefer not to get out there to talk to customers or staff as they might tell us uncomfortable truths, sometimes about ourselves; or these activities are a way for us to get a bit of time-out from the pressure of the business; or time in the office makes us feel important; or we're doing it because of the owners' or bankers' requirements.

The most important people in the business are the customers and the staff, and time spent away from them should be grudged.

I'm not talking about the tokenism of managers spending one week a year stacking shelves. I'm talking about how, in the 21st century, we can all take the laptop and go and work anywhere. So, take your laptop and sit down everywhere in your business – be visible and accessible. And also ask your customers if you can spend time working at their premises, if appropriate.

All of this really matters, and it deserves all of the time that you can invest in it. What better way do you have to learn about what is really going on and what is important?

And, while you're at it, boot your team out of their offices as well, perhaps even closing some of the offices down. They need to get out as well.

7) Screw-ups aren't welcome or enjoyable but..........

It's impossible to get it right all the time for customers, so all managers have to deal with problems on a regular basis.

Problems are never welcome, but they are sometimes the best opportunity you will ever have to create real long-term customer loyalty, and be different from the competition. . Most customers value highly a supplier who apologises and takes responsibility, and then totally exceeds expectations to fix an issue.

I had a problem in a business where we automatically telephone surveyed customers of a major global blue chip customer – sadly, we called 800 people at 1 o'clock in the morning. Naturally, it all kicked off the next day and, after some discussion, we were asked to fund firstly £10, then £20 compensation per customer.

In that situation, the reaction of most businesses is firstly to try to avoid or spread around the blame; and then to find ways to reduce the costs of the credit note or to put things right.

After much heart-searching, our inspired response was to say "let's make it £25, we care about your customers at least as much as you do." Over the following 18 months, our business with that customer more than doubled to a £10m account! When you find a supplier who thinks and behaves like that, most customers want to hang on to them; it's so different!

I realised afterwards that spending money on creating a compelling customer experience, following a screw-up, was just another form of marketing spend; and a much better way to spend the marketing budget than the usual traditional ways of sports or social events, and alcohol!

Actually, any money that you spend that affects your customers should be treated as marketing spend and focused on delivering a great Customer Experience, making the customers say "wow" and showing the difference between you and the competition.

Setting part of the marketing budget to one side, to create these ad-hoc experiences, might be a very smart move indeed.

8) **The importance of Thinking; use your brain!**

30 years ago, when I first started in business, car journeys were great – there were no mobile phones, no wireless internet, even the radio was dull. So, for that 2 or 3 hours' journey, or that one hour commute, you were cut off from your normal hurly-burly.

What this meant was that you had the time to think; not just time to think, but time to think in a leisurely way (maybe even daydream), without any time pressure. And so there could be some really deep thinking and some high quality creative thinking – use of the imagination!

The end result was often that you could get in your car with a problem and have the solution, or at least a range of good ideas, by the end of the journey.

Today, the opportunity for managers to have that quality of thinking time has been taken away. We save up our phone calls for when we are in the car or on the train; the phone is always switched on so we are always available; even if we don't answer the phone, we're doing e-mails in meetings, on our smartphones or IPAD's – people are "chronically busy" and "chronically fast" in a way that feels like a form of mental illness. We create an environment of speed and constant interruption, and this prevents deep, slow, productive thinking and ensures that our thinking, if it even takes place, is at best shallow.

What's more, our colleagues reinforce these problems: we are expected by them to be always "available" and "contactable"; people assume, if they've sent you an e-mail, that you "know about it", and immediately.

So, the quality of management thinking is much poorer than it used to be; it's too rushed, reflecting the lack of time and the need of managers to find instant solutions all the time.

You have to resist all of this and find strategies that work for you to give the time to get the best out of your most important organ (no, I mean your brain, actually!).

So: switch off your phone (especially in the car), be unavailable at certain times in the week, don't look at your e-mails more than 3 times a day; be out of your office regularly, and sometimes out of the work-place.

Take back the quality, uncontrolled, slow time that you need to carry out one of the most important management activities – high quality THINKING!

9) You have to become Different, Special and Unique — and that will involve breaking the rules in your sector.

Different – not like the mainstream

Special – worth more to customers and staff

Unique – the only one; no one else like us

There's no point in being like most other businesses; if you are like that, then the way that you will win and keep business is likely to be on price, with lower margins.

And that means your business risks becoming progressively commoditised by aggressive B2B procurement teams, most of whom believe that all suppliers are really the same and who are bonused on cost reductions. Or, if you are a B2C business, your customers will victimise you by looking always for the cheapest headline price.

So, you have to find ways to be Different; better still to go beyond that, to be Special to your customers and your people; best of all to become Unique – to have something that the customers want badly and they can't easily get anywhere else. That's what really makes them stick to you, as they can't and don't want to go anywhere else.

I've seen this delivered in all manner of ways:

- An extreme commitment to Customer Experience and Service, that matters to the customers you want; Being the Best by far in looking after customers.
- A continual flow of innovation and new ideas for customers, backed by a powerful technology team.
- A willingness to design and deliver on commercial models that match customer needs, rather than supplier preferences (albeit you have to make decent money).
- Designs that can't be found elsewhere.
- Performance levels beyond those found anywhere else.
- A full range of services that are available in one place – one-stop shop.
- Being Different in small but powerful ways, such as sending round branded cakes to customers, or running Ladies' Days for female customers in male-dominated industries!

You could easily expand this list with your own thoughts, but the bottom-line is that you have at least to be Different if you are going to make serious money in your business and create a great future for yourself and your staff. Being Different can be implemented at every level of your business and team, as it's often the small differences that mean the most to customers and which they really notice.

Different certainly means spending less time thinking about the competition, as you are not trying to be like them.

And even if you are Different, Special and Unique, there will still be procurement people (often from big blue chips) who will want to treat your business as if it is just another commoditised supplier. But once you are confident that you have something that people want badly and can't easily get anywhere else, then learn to politely say "no" to the procurement people.

Ultimately, you may even need to plan your exit from those customers who will never want to offer any extra value for what you have, when you've found new customers who do value it. If you have become Different, Special and Unique, then you deserve to generate great returns for all stakeholders.

10) Authenticity; you need to be yourself, but more perfectly

Authenticity (being yourself; being genuine) is one of the hardest things for managers to deliver, but crucial.

Authentic leaders are genuine people who are true to themselves and what they believe in. They engender trust and develop genuine connections to others. Rather than letting the expectations of others guide them, they aim to be themselves and go their own way, even if that may have painful consequences.

People will only trust you in the long-term when you are genuine and authentic, not an imitation. And trust is essential for leaders and managers in business, as all leadership depends ultimately on the consent and belief of those being led, which flows from trust.

However, to be truly yourself, you have to understand firstly who you are, and your life story – how you got to where you are today – and to learn to like and value yourself. All leaders should work hard on this.

I finally got this point a few years ago on a team Away Day. The consultant running the day showed 2 opposing lists of the characteristics of leaders:

- True Self; positive qualities that all leaders/managers should want to have.
- Ego; every characteristic the opposite of True Self, or defeating True Self.

What I realised was that the qualities of True Self were the qualities that I aspired to as a manager and, critically, these were the real me, but my behaviours (driven by personality, history, poor role models etc) were actually leading me to show the characteristics of Ego.

This then caused me to think deeply about what my own behaviours were doing to me and, even worse, what I was doing to other people.

The realisation of who you really are as a person, and as a leader/manager, is the starting point to becoming authentic in your behaviours and reaping the benefits in business.

And no-one can be authentic by trying to be like some-one else; you can learn from others' experiences and adapt those learnings to yourself, but you cannot be wholly successful by trying to be like others.

You don't actually have be like other people, you just have to be like your real self, <u>but more perfectly</u> than you are doing today.

11) There is no universal style of successful leadership

A related truth to the subject of the previous chapter on authenticity is that there is no universal style of successful leadership.

Over the last 30 years, I seem to have met every style of successful leader and manager – loud, quiet, enthusiastic, calm/introverted, formal, informal, technology driven, technology illiterate, male, female, and from every ethnic background.

So, there is no universal style that works well in all situations, although different challenges may benefit more from different styles, and leaders need to learn and practise different approaches to different situations.

This then means that pretty much every type of personality and style can become a great leader in the right circumstances and with the right support. That being the case, you might as well concentrate on learning who you are and becoming that person more perfectly, working to hone the principal leadership style that is really you, and which you can make the most effective use of.

Although there is no universal style of successful leadership, unsurprisingly there are some common features to all great leaders and managers.

One of the most important of these is that they are passionate about what they are doing – the business that they are building and the people that they are working with. So find a business that really motivates you if you want to maximise your chances of developing your leadership capability.

And find people who you are motivated to work with.

12) Strategy nonsense; you need a simple vision

Nearly all of the strategy exercises that I've been involved in turn out, at worst, to have been largely nonsense, a waste of time and demoralising for the staff, or at best neutral.

Typically, what happens is that the CEO and his team (and often some consultants who know very little about the business) shut themselves up in a project over a period of months (or even more than a year).

Sometimes these exercises develop into a form of pantomime, such as when a consultant (a man with white frizzy hair) urged the senior team of which I was a part, to hop around the room making frog noises; apparently this was to help us to think more creatively. You just couldn't make it up!

The end result is then launched to the company with road shows and razzmatazz. An enormous strategy document is produced, riddled with management-speak and inaccessible to most of the staff.

12 months later, most of the company can't tell you what the strategy is (assuming they ever could) or, more relevantly, what they are doing about it. The strategy ends up as a document

that gathers dust on executive shelves and has no impact on the daily running of the business. It's then superseded by another exercise, often led by the next CEO; eventually, after a few iterations, people lose confidence in these exercises and they become even less of value.

A successful strategy is one that creates a very simple vision that the whole company can be motivated by and get on board with – deciding for themselves how it can be implemented, making it their own. The right strategy creates unity of purpose (although not uniformity).

Therefore it must be simple – in the plainest possible English, and very short. Otherwise, most people in your business will not know or understand it; and they will then not own it, and cannot implement it successfully. We all know that most great businesses are simple – so why should strategy be complex?

A good test of any strategy is to go round a business and ask random staff at all levels 2 simple questions:

- What is the strategy of this business?
- What actions are you taking in your daily work to deliver the strategy?

In my experience, the responses are usually blank faces, or confusion!

13) What might a simple strategy look like?

Given that a simple strategy is easy to understand and act on, creating that strategy might seem at first to be straightforward.

However, my experience has been that making something simple is one of the hardest things to do in a business. So, let me offer you a template approach, to help your thinking, that took me years to develop but which has worked well for me.

I now regularly use a 3 point approach to strategy that answers the following questions:

- **What do we do?** A brief 20-30 word description of our services.
- **How do we want to do it?** Typically, we answer this by saying that "we want to Be the Best", that is great Value For Money. I've always avoided strategies aimed at being the cheapest, the "drive to the bottom".
- **How do we want to do it with Customers?** A regular answer here is to say that "we want to do everything the Customers want <u>and more</u>. We want to make our Customers feel Great and, by doing that, make our staff feel Great".

Basically, these 3 points comprise the entire strategy and are all I expect the staff to know and to be putting into action.

The consequences of this strategy are two-fold:

- The kind of business we become (usually a 20-30 word statement about quality and reputation); and
- The financial by-products of becoming that business – in terms of sales, profits and cash flows.

Note that the financial results are the by-product of the kind of business and people we become; they are not, unlike in many companies, the strategy itself. I think that if you have the right strategy and execute it well, the numbers take care of themselves.

Note also that just because these statements are simple doesn't mean that they are not deep and rich and pregnant with meaning. My experience is that people can embrace the strategy as a framework for detailed and sophisticated plans for their areas. The strategy is the glue that holds their plan together and holds the whole business together.

14) Strategy; the power of the many

Let's return to simplicity - we've been discussing how a strategy needs to be simple, to get people on board.

The importance of this lies in the "power of many" people moving as one. If you can get most staff bought into the strategy, understanding and making it theirs, working it and generating action – then the power of those many people becomes irresistible as they drive forward in the direction set out by the strategy, taking everyone along with them. Very few things are as powerful in business as this.

And as success starts to happen, then a surge of confidence goes through the whole business as everyone (including some initial detractors) sees that this is the way to success, and everyone wants to get on board and do more of it.

Your strategy will then become the means to create an environment in your business or team, in which all or most of the people feel like using their brains, hands and talent to help the business or team Become the Best it can be.

So how do you facilitate this? Once you have the simple strategy, that's only the start.

The main lesson I've learnt is that you have to keep repeating the strategy to people until it sinks in and keep testing and challenging that it has, getting them to play it back to you; constant repetition is a fundamental but underrated management tool, if people are to learn the strategy and never forget it.

At the same time, you must require your staff to put the strategy into action as part of their personal objectives and departmental plans, to work out for themselves what it means, to generate good ideas for implementing it. Once they know the strategy and see its value as they put it into action, they'll want to do more.

Crucially, as part of this, you must also give away as much power as possible over the strategy of the business – not to allow people to alter it (once agreed), but to give them power over how it's implemented. And that means allowing, within reason and with support, your people to make choices that wouldn't be your own; looking for the bigger gain that comes from empowering them and getting them to see the strategy as their own; with the opportunity to get so much more out of their working lives if they really get behind it and deliver it.

Strategies are usually executed when the "power of the many" gets going, so, give away some of your power to your people to deliver the strategy and watch them get cracking!

15) The whole team must join in (See your staff as an army on the march)

This point about getting as many people as possible to embrace the vision and to work cooperatively to take a business forward, and how to do this, is something that took me a long time to fully learn in business; but it's crucial to all parts of a business, not just strategy.

The mind-set I used to have was one of "I might as well do it myself", or irritation with other people's "sub-standard efforts", or just wanting to have the credit myself.

I started to learn this lesson as a CFO. We were under severe pressure to cut costs and repay banking and I was struggling to see how we could make it through; so, I had an idea to put a whiteboard outside my office and ask every member of the team to come up with at least one idea, no matter how small, to save money or generate cash flow. Key features of the whiteboard, developed over a lot of learning, were:

- Writing on the whiteboard was in front of the office, visible to very one and you had to put your name against it, so everyone knew who had put forward the idea.

- Initially some people were shy, but I worked to get everyone doing it, even suggesting possibilities to people who were struggling to get started ("gimmes") and giving away the credit to people for ideas that were really more my own.
- At the end of the month, we celebrated the ideas with prizes, and I went through and publicly praised <u>every</u> idea and <u>everyone</u> else I could.
- Once this got going, the whole team joined in; even visitors starting chipping in with their own thoughts!

We recorded the ideas on a spreadsheet. Over 4 years, the whiteboard generated £20m of cost savings and cash flow improvements, in a business with £30m sales. Even better, it helped to trigger a transformation in attitude and atmosphere in the team, as people saw that they could make a difference and be appreciated and recognised for it. Eventually, the full team took ownership of the whiteboard and I became a bit player in it.

That's when I started to learn about the "power of the many"; if you can see your team as an army (after all, business is a form of warfare!) and get them all pointing and marching in the same direction, they become unstoppable and the results can exceed all expectations.

Once you really get going with this, you can ask your people for all of their other ideas and they will also start to come forward without being asked. People just need to feel that they have something to contribute and that they can really make a difference; and when they do put something forward, it must be celebrated and recognised, so they feel good about it and want to do it again, as well as encouraging others to join in.

It's amazing what intelligence and creativity is lying dormant in people in most businesses, just wanting to be let loose and given a chance.

Let's therefore explore even more fully two of the themes we've just mentioned - giving away the credit for success and giving away power - in the next chapters, as they relate to more than just the strategy of a business.

16) Give away the credit for everything

As we've touched on earlier, a vital part of getting your team and staff energised and united behind you as leader is to make sure you give away all of the credit; and I mean <u>all</u> of it. As a manager, success should be much more interesting to you than personal praise.

This lesson applies to more than just the strategy exercise we discussed previously; most business success is going to come through your team.

It's a real temptation when things are going well to take or accept the credit and revel in the glory; do that, and you will miss a great chance to motivate your team on to the next level.

Managers should treat any public credit they are given as something they need to get rid of <u>immediately</u> to their teams, publicly giving the recognition to teams and individuals who they want to motivate.

One of the main things that people want from their work is to feel appreciated, valued and important — just like customers — and that's something that modern business life doesn't always provide. Business is full of instances where some-one in a team comes up with an idea or does something good and they find that their manager or some-one else has "taken the credit". How does that make them feel and how does it affect their future approach? So give the credit away, all of it, as soon as you can.

When you, as manager, get the credit for something in your team, treat it as a great opportunity to give it to your people and to make them feel good about themselves; if you do that, they will pay you back many times over in terms of loyalty, support and even more good ideas. People like people who make them look good and it's especially powerful if people know you are being generous and that you also ought to be taking some of the credit.

Giving away the credit for success to your peer group and boss is also a smart thing to do.

All of this is closely related to the idea that directors and managers are mainly there to serve; that the higher you go up an organisation, the more you are there to serve.

Let others have the public credit. Everyone knows anyway who really is delivering!

17) While you're at it, give away power as well

Another thing that managers often find hard, but need to learn, is to give away their own power.....to their team.

There's a lot of talk in modern management theory about "empowering people" – a real b*ll*cks phrase, it sounds like you are plugging the staff into the electricity supply! What it really means is giving your people power and, in order to do that, you have to give away <u>your own</u> power, as the power you are giving to people doesn't come out of thin air.

I've been repeating myself quite a bit on this, but it's crucial to successful management and not enough is seen of it in real action, beyond plenty of lip service, waffle and PowerPoint presentations about "empowering people".

Younger or newer managers find giving away their power particularly hard to do. After all that hard work, effort, brown-nosing and playing the corporate game, they've finally achieved their heart's desire – the power, the status, the recognition of being a manager. Then people like me are telling them to give some of it away. They must think I am mad (or perhaps just getting a bit senile!).

But, if you are going to create the "power of the many", one of the starting points is to give the team more of your own power. That means trusting people with their own projects and responsibilities, then closing your eyes (but with some judicious hands-off monitoring) and letting them learn how to do it, with all the failures and trial and error that this involves. And then dealing with any problems that arise, knowing that you probably could have done a better job yourself. But they will learn so much more from the experience, and that will benefit both them and you and the business going forward.

As much as anything, this giving away power is about trust – essential in any team and core to the relationship between a manager and his staff. Like power, trust also does not appear out of thin air and it starts by some-one taking a bit of a risk. Some-one has to make the first move and trust, and it might as well be you, since you're the leader! And, if it doesn't work the first time, you will have to find a way to force yourself to trust that person again in the future, or they will never learn to be the person they could be for you and the business. Or they will have to be replaced, if you can't trust them.

How else are your people going to grow and learn and develop, and create the great team that you aspire to be the leader of – unless you are prepared to take controlled risks and trust them with some of your power, with all the benefit that accrues when your staff see that you are trusting them?

Curiously, it's one of the more interesting discoveries of modern management theory that the more power you can give away, judiciously and thoughtfully, the more powerful a leader you can become yourself. Think hard about the truth in this, if you really want to be a great leader.

18) Gloat over the positive feedback you receive

I talked in a previous chapter about how important it is to try to give away to your team all of the credit, but I was talking about the public credit only.

It's also important in private to <u>gloat</u>, yes gloat, over the positive feedback that you receive.

We're all human and part of that humanity is that leaders and managers also need to feel appreciated and valued ourselves. In giving away all of the credit to your teams, you can also neglect your own needs.

So, in private, regularly go over the successes that you have achieved and savour every part of the experience; also use it as an opportunity to review exactly why you were successful, and to think about how to reinforce those learnings and repeat the success.

Use your achievements to feel good about yourself and to build the emotional platform for the next success.

There's nothing wrong with, and everything good about, feeling good about yourself!

19) You get more out of people by being positive with them

A simple truth that took me a long time to really understand.

As a young manager, I used to hand out the bad stuff far too readily, and sometimes in public which is even worse.

Most people want to be appreciated and valued; they want to do a good job and they want to feel good as a result.

So, words and phrases like "thanks for your terrific efforts" and "well done" should be used regularly, and in front of as many people as possible.

You must find ways to be positive with people, even if your starting point is celebrating mediocrity. What's mediocre for you may well be a great achievement for some-one else and the starting point on their journey to be better.

If you are struggling to find something credible about their work to praise, you're probably not looking hard enough – everyone does good things; or maybe you can find something good about them outside of work that you've heard about. Praising people is a sure way to get their positive juices flowing.

And when you praise people, make sure you do it in a way that other people get to know about it. And do it in as authentic a way as possible, make it obviously sincere and genuine.

Also, provided people have the right attitude and desire to learn, aim to be lenient and generous with them as they start to learn, until they have the confidence to bear tougher lessons. Learning not to comment on every mistake or weakness was a big step forward for me in management.

This is important for all ages of people, but particularly true of young people, whose home and school environment may mean that they've never before had some-one to believe in them.

Praise and appreciation are crucial tools in the great manager's toolkit, to win people's hearts and minds, to get them to commit to the cause, and to start to unlock the potential inside of them that is often hidden through their own lack of self-belief and confidence.

One final point: you may say that you personally find it hard to praise people sincerely, it's not you. My response: <u>force yourself to start doing it</u>. Giving out praise doesn't just help those who are receiving the praise; it also changes the people who are giving it out, and it changes them for the good as well.

20) Be kinder to other points of view

An area of positivity that will pay real dividends in businesses and teams is your treatment of people who you disagree with.

Too often leaders and managers treat disagreements as a war in which the other side has to lose the argument and more. I know that's how I've behaved in the past often, not only wanting to win the argument, but doing so in a way that makes the other person feel worse about themselves. I often won arguments, but lost so much more.

When you disagree with some-one in your team, some key things to remember:

- You actually want people to tell you when they disagree with you, not to clam up because of the risk in telling you. Otherwise, how are you personally going to learn and make better decisions?
- Remember, when you are running a team, it's about the "power of the many", not about you.
- Very few decisions are black and white; so you need to see the truth in other people's views as it may influence what needs to be done.
- The success of most decisions is heavily influenced by how enthusiastically it's

implemented; a mediocre decision that everyone gets behind can often produce an outstanding result, whereas the reverse can be true of a great decision that lacks active buy-in from the wider team.

So, make sure you are kinder to points of view that you don't agree with, your objective being to ensure that people feel it was worthwhile contributing and want to do it again; and to give their all to support the decision that was actually made.

21) There's no point in not trying to Be the Best that you can be

In some businesses I've been involved with, we've had a company objective of trying to Be the Best that we can be; this also affected the kind of people we wanted in the business – only people who wanted to Be the Best.

Being the Best is a mind-set that is relevant to every employee in the business – right down to the person who cleans the toilets, who also makes a difference to how your company is regarded.

Being the Best is not about the egoism of being no 1 all the time, as that's impossible and leads often to corrosive behaviours; it's about a mind-set of always <u>wanting</u> to Be the Best - continually striving to learn and improve, and to give it everything you have, working well with colleagues as part of a team.

If you go round private businesses and the public sector in the UK, they're often full of people who only want to be average, people who want to do their minimum hours, with average effort, and nothing more. These organisations are ultimately doomed as, out there, there are others who are faster, more determined and more committed to Being the Best

You have to ask why organisations employ people like this and what it is in the culture of the organisation that allows people like this be accepted and to stay.

You also need to question the poverty of ambition of people whose aspiration for their jobs is to only do the minimum, and then stop. We spend more of our waking lives in work than in any other activity, so we ought to expect a lot more from it than just a job and salary, in terms of success and personal satisfaction.

If many of us carry on accepting a second-rate view of what work should mean for us, not only are our businesses doomed, but our country is also doomed to be second-rate against the aggressive new economies and work-forces in the developing world.

If, however, you can turn this around and infect people with the idea that Being the Best is what they are entitled to expect from their jobs, then you have a real chance; if everyone in the company starts to think like this, it creates that unstoppable force that we've been discussing in previous chapters. And what is true for a company can be true on a much bigger scale.

So, get out there and make it clear what the standard is in your team – the only people you want are people who want to Be the Best!

22) Do <u>more</u> than the customers expect

Another important part of the culture of a successful business is to have this simple idea in all of your people's heads – "I'll find out what our customers want, and I'll check with them that we are providing it; then, preferably based on what I know about them as a business and as individuals, I'll think of <u>something extra</u> that we can do for them that they weren't expecting, that will surprise and impress them".

"Everything the customers want, <u>and more</u>" – it's a simple concept to understand but one with real power, that most businesses aren't doing.

Most businesses are just trying to do what their customers want and no more, which makes them the same as the competition, with no compelling reason for the customers to deal with one supplier rather than another.

Amazingly, a lot of businesses, in the current climate, are trying to do even less than the customers want, trying first to satisfy their accountants' need to balance the cost books, rather than focusing on the real priority, their customers. Those businesses are often engaged in ongoing battles with customers who feel short-changed by the service; the businesses lose far more than the costs they save and the profits keep going backwards, making the bean-counters even unhappier.

A surprising thing about doing "everything the customers want <u>and more</u>" is how small the little touches can be to make that difference but, as long as there is a difference, you're ahead of the competition and customers do notice.

Another amazing thing about this approach is the power in a customer's mind of something that they like, but they weren't expecting and, even better, they know that you didn't need to do; it shows them that you do genuinely care about them and that they are your top priority.

You end up not only with delighted customers who keep coming back, but also ones who are happy to recommend you to their friends and colleagues. Delighted customers are the most powerful sales force you will ever have.

Doing "everything the customer wants <u>and more</u>" is the only way to great and long-lasting customer relationships.

It's also very smart business.

23) Customers only really trust suppliers who are genuinely unselfish

Businesses today talk a lot about "partnering" with customers and being trusted by them; yet most B2B or B2C customers see their suppliers' interest in them as driven solely by the selfish desire to make money – "they are only talking to me because they want to sell me something" - and give them the loyalty they deserve.

Consider this customer feedback given to me:

- Your people only call me when they want something.
- When something has gone wrong, your people don't return my calls; when we do get hold of them, their first reaction is to try to evade responsibility.
- When we're not buying, you're not interested in us.

This feedback is clear evidence of selfishness, yet my business talked all the time about "partnering" with its customers. Sounds familiar?

Now compare this behaviour to what we did later when a major blue chip client had a serious technical issue that was preventing it from handing thousands of daily customer contacts. The client rang in a panic asking what we could do. From a standing start, our teams worked through the night and, by the next day, were handling hundreds of contacts.

At the end of the month, I get a call from the client saying how delighted their main Board were with our response and asking me what we were going to invoice for it – to which I say "nothing"; invoicing them had never occurred to me – I just saw it as a great opportunity to show them we really cared. We then have a bizarre conversation about how every other supplier who helped has billed them triple-time; the client then ends up ordering me to invoice them X% extra that month; I reluctantly agree.

3 years later, the account had gone from £10m to £30m and the customer was still telling people "you'd never believe what they did when we had that problem – they are like no-one else I've done business with".

So, think about ways in which you can be genuinely unselfish with customers – doing things with and for them where there is no immediate commercial gain. The customers you want will understand and value you accordingly.

Consider it just another form of marketing.

24) Living up to your brand

A useful exercise, connected with Customer Experience, is to check the websites of the UK businesses that you yourself are a customer of, in order to list out the brand promises that they are making to their customers. Promises like:

- Speed and simplicity
- We'll "be easy to deal with" and "be there when you need us"
- It's all about trust
- Customers trust us to take care of their needs
- People use us because of our reputation for plain speaking

Then assess to what extent these stated brand values are really a part of the DNA of the businesses, and how that affects your attitude and loyalty to them as a supplier.

When doing this, focus on how these businesses behave when things are not going right. Most businesses deliver their brand values when things have gone smoothly. But both people and businesses show their real underlying values when it isn't going well and the pressure is on.

An underlying truth here is that the only consistent promise that many businesses keep with their customers is the unspoken one to "sweat the maximum profit out of them at every point in the customer lifecycle."

Customers are not the fools that many businesses think they are. They see through business behaviour like this and the suppliers get the customers, and the customer loyalty and attitudes, they deserve.

The saddest part of all is that the companies often have no idea as the extent and cost of these attitudes – senior management think they are being smart; but the customers have no interest in telling them the truth, although they always tell other customers.

Once you've done this exercise and are feeling a little bit smug, apply the same process to the brand values that your own company promotes in public and the brand values that you yourself set out as your personal promise to others.

Then consider the real impact you are having on your company's and your own customers, to the extent that you don't live up to the values that are being proclaimed.

Just think what they might be thinking of you…..at this very moment! And then make the changes.

25) Large scale change is often the result of a series of smaller changes

Managers today are usually under huge pressure to make big improvements quickly – "we need a big quick win".

Usually, this pressure comes from shareholders or bankers who don't understand the business at all and have no concept that long-term sustainable business success requires both time and investment to create. Sometimes, they not only don't understand but they don't care (usually because of the pressures they themselves are under) – they don't want a manager, they want a magician (or con artist) who will produce a quick solution to the pain, or a quick increase in profitability, that they can then sell the business off the back of; when that doesn't work, they then look for and get another snake-oil salesman in as CEO. That's why the longevity of most CEO's is around 2 years – they didn't produce the quick smoke and mirrors act that their masters required!

All of this pressure ultimately is most likely to reduce or destroy stakeholder value because of the way that managers respond to the pressure. And the shareholders may not even know, because they never saw or understood what it could have been like if they've behaved differently.

Under-pressure managers tend to look for that one big quick fix and forget the lessons of the "power of the many" described in the previous chapters, and the related lesson that most large scale long-term business improvement is the result of a lot of small changes (and a few big ones) generated by many people getting on board and driving towards a common objective.

Of course, big changes do matter, but I've been amazed as to how many small changes can add up to big sums. Even better, small changes have the benefit of giving everyone an opportunity to get on board and thereby make change irresistible and permanent, as well as everywhere in your business.

So, don't turn your nose up at the smaller changes/improvements. I have a notice on my door which says "what have you done today to make this business better". If I can positively answer this question every day or at least once every week, even if the individual improvement is small, then the effect over a year will be enormous.

If, as well as doing this yourself, you can influence people in your team and business to think the same way, and for them to influence their teams, then together you become unstoppable.

26) Most management truth is simple, but you need to think deeply, slowly and long about it, and spend time putting it into action.

If you're still with me at this stage in the book, you'll have noticed that we are talking about some fairly simple stuff, in the plainest possible English.

That's because the most important and worthwhile truths about management and leadership are simple to express and understand.

There are whole libraries of nonsense written about management and business success, in terms that are inaccessible except to the initiated (consultants and MBA's and the like), or those who buy their courses and books.

Yet, the truths about how to be successful remain largely unchanged, even though the cultural context and specific management issues may vary.

With so much of this type of material around, one of the biggest dangers is for managers (particularly the younger ones) is to drown in the jargon; or to flit around like butterflies, searching asking for that quick miracle fix that will deliver short-term gains.......a bit like shareholders looking for great CEO's, actually!

In most cases, what you need comes from deep, slow, long, personal thinking about the few key simple truths in this book, and then learning by putting them into action over a long period. You need to stay on these individual truths for a long time to get the full value out of them and, crucially, to make them your own – by experimenting and learning to deliver them in your own way.

Don't be a butterfly – flitting quickly from one new thing to another.

If you can just find 3 or 4 major truths in this book that really matter to you, and then spend 12 months learning to put them fully and completely and vigorously into action, then studying this book will have been well worth your effort (and well worth my writing it).

You can then ignore all the other chapters for the time being, as you have already plenty to think about and do in the next 12 months!

27) If people are never going to be good enough, sort them out as soon as possible

There are plenty of these people around, who haven't been sorted out.

People who just cannot do their jobs, yet who may have been in the same team for years; this can be for all kinds of reasons: they have just been there too long and have never been performance managed properly; they have a connection of some kind to senior people; they are liked as people, even though they can't do the job; they could do damage to the business if exited; no practical support from HR for action etc etc.

Whatever the reason is, they have to be managed like anyone else and, if they can't do their jobs or be trained to do it, they have to be exited and quickly!

Seems easy and straightforward doesn't it? But this country is full of people in jobs they can't do with many bad consequences:

- Damage to their company (and to everyone's job security!).
- Undermining of the credibility of the manager in the eyes of the rest of the team;

everyone in a team knows if they have a passenger who is not being dealt with.
- The standard of the whole team being lowered, as people assume they just need to be better than the passenger, since he/she's the next one out and he/she therefore sets the minimum standard for the rest.
- The employee involved being made miserable. In most cases, they know that they can't do their job, and that people around them know this; therefore, they suffer from a lack of self-respect and, effectively, the way that they are being treated is cruel. Think about this: one of the cruellest things you can do to your staff is to leave them in a job that everyone knows they can't do.
- Even more cruel, by the inaction of the manager, nearly always meant to be kindly, the employee is prevented from going out actively to find the job that they can do. Everyone has talent, a lot of people are just wasting their lives in the wrong job and ending up miserable, as a result. Good managers help people like that to be on their way and thereby to move forward.

In the long-term, some people will actually thank you if you get them out of a job they can't do; it is usually the trigger for opportunities and decisions that they themselves were unable to make on their own.

And, of course, the longer you don't face up to the problem, the worse it gets for everyone.

So, if you are a manager, face up to the people in your team who are not doing their jobs, start to performance manage them now (to see if they really are beyond recovery) and start to plan for their exit and replacement, if they can't be turned around.

This is just doing the decent thing, both for the person involved and for the sake of other staff whose jobs and prospects rely on you doing your job – managing.

Easy, isn't it? So, just get on with it, please!

28) Sometimes people are just in the wrong job, or have never been properly managed or given a chance

But just before you leap up and fire all your non-performers, learn and consider carefully also why these people aren't doing their jobs; it may be that, with proper performance management and coaching, their talents will come through; or, it may be they are genuinely talented, but in another job in your business, and you'd be a fool to let them go.

The advice in the last chapter was not to throw people overboard immediately, but to face up to non-performance and act immediately......using the performance management and improvement processes in your business.

As well as seeing many people in jobs that they currently were unable to do, I've also seen enough people who were just being very badly managed, or not being managed; with the right support and the belief of their managers, some of these people eventually were amongst the most remarkable and talented people I've ever worked with; and, as a manager, there's no bigger kick than to be a part of such a transformation.

Many benefits result from this:

- You save on replacement costs.
- You discover how remarkable talent can be hidden out of sight.
- Your whole team see how you are willing to positively invest in people, and they respond to your leadership.
- The employee who has been turned around, knows the debt they owe, and rewards you with intense loyalty.

So, go to it and discover what amazing people you have in your team.

Equally, once you know that some-one is unlikely to ever reach the required standard, then they have to go (with dignity and respect), don't they? You haven't got any more time to invest in them and the rest of your team need you as well.

29) The most unpromising materials can sometimes be moulded

Thinking further about the last chapter and my own experience, it's a big surprise how bad some of the very best people I've worked with actually looked, when I first came across them.

A number of them I would normally have actually fired immediately but, through circumstances or other reasons, wasn't able to act on the initial impression. That would have been a big mistake, as they proved in the end to be truly remarkable and outstanding people.

It's actually quite amazing how much talent, creativity and all round ability there is out there. It just needs somebody (their manager) to help these people to show their true selves, no matter how bad they might look at the start. Sometimes just painting a picture in people's minds of the person they are going to be, and reminding them of that regularly, is enough to drive them forward to success.

Another important factor is the impact on people when they know that their manager believes in them, trusts in them and is relying on them. It's astonishing how many people have never had anyone to really believe in them, not just in work but throughout their lives. I've great memories of how some of the most exceptional managers I've ever worked with have come from very deprived and challenging backgrounds, where no-one believed in them. Indeed the culture made them believe that they would never be good enough to achieve anything worthwhile. So, the uplift when someone finally did believe in them was both dramatic and very powerful.

How you deal with these unpromising materials is important; it's a key measure for me of the success of any manager as a team-builder; comparing the team they created to the team they actually started with, and therefore how far they were able to take their people.

Once this happened to me – someone believed in me, when I didn't look at all the part, and gave me an opportunity, creating the belief in myself that was essential for success. Thanks to you - for giving me my chance. Mind you, I know you were out of decent alternatives at the time!

I hope that, at critical moments in your career, people will believe in you, and give you your chance too.

30) Desire is everything

So, when you are looking at your team and trying to work out who is worth investing in and who needs to go, how do you make up your mind?

It's desire that I'm always looking for – the feeling that some-one will do pretty much anything legal and decent to make the grade and succeed: they will stay late, they will learn and they are willing to change, they want to take the pain and pay the price of growth, they are resilient and bounce back after a bad time, they go the extra mile – doing everything you expect and then some more.

You see, desire will beat talent nearly every time; I'll go even further than that and say that desire creates talent. I've had some amazingly talented people working with me, but they weren't at all talented when we started – they just became talented along the way, through their desire to succeed and what they did to learn how to succeed!

Some people say that character is what counts, but desire is more important as it creates character through experiences. Desire comes first.

Desire changes people and makes things happen. It underpins all kinds of crucial and positive characteristics in business – not just talent, but also fortitude and persistence and endurance.

So, the main thing you need to know about your staff is "how badly does he/she want to succeed and will he/she pay the price?" And find ways to ramp up that desire to white-hot levels.

And, in respect of your own self, working on ways to supercharge the level of your own desire – to turn a small fire into a raging inferno – will only reap dividends for you too. Desire is fundamental to your own success as well.

31) Hard work

One of the best ways to spot the people who have the necessary desire is to see who is putting the effort in.

You see, an important output of desire is hard work. This, and the sacrifices associated with it, are essential components of success.

I remember one evening being in the office with our most successful salesperson – a lady in her twenties who was earning twice the money of the next sales person in the league tables.

When she had put the phone down from speaking to a customer, I asked her, "Jane, what is the secret of your success in sales?"

She looked at me and said, "It's 8 o'clock on a Friday evening, Mark; what do you see". I said I see you and I see me, on our own, and the office"; to which she replied, "that's the only secret of my success, I just try harder than anyone else here; the first couple of years, I thought I would lose my job, as nothing seemed to work; but I kept on trying and trying, and working harder and longer than anyone else; then, once I started to make the sales, I couldn't be stopped.

All of the success I've had needed to be earned in advance."

I think that story sums it up for most of us. There are lottery winners around in business, people who were lucky and didn't have to work for it. But, in general, hard graft over a long period is the foundation of nearly all business success.

The workers are the winners.

So let's get cracking and keep going.

32) You have to know your people as people

We've talked a lot in the previous chapters about making decisions about people.

These decisions are always judgement calls – because people are people. So, you can and will get them wrong from time to time. I know I get this area wrong regularly! But you can radically improve your chances of getting these decisions right by getting to know your people…….by that I mean really getting to know them – what makes them tick, what do they feel about the company, their jobs and you, what their home lives are like etc.

And to get to know them properly, you really must care about them and regard them as more than just pawns on the business chessboard.

You can be tough as a leader and yet still care deeply about your people.

A leader who genuinely cares, and is seen to care, gets much more loyalty and support, and stands a far better chance of multiplying the power of himself and his team.

People today demand and expect a level of personal relationship with their leaders before they will give the commitment and loyalty that leaders need from them.

33) Great managers lose their people

Here's another contradiction to most managers' thinking – the best ones lose their senior people.

When you hear that "John has a fantastic team – they have all been with him for 10 years", it may not actually reflect well on John. It could easily mean:

- John never developed his senior people so they could get promoted; he never gave them the chance to move beyond him.
- No-one wants to poach any of his senior people, because they aren't that good or they lack ambition.
- John has no succession planning – so he can't afford to let anyone go.
- After 10 years, John's team has gone stale; it's him who needs to move on.
- The more junior staff know that their only chance to get on is to go elsewhere. So, John's senior people are never challenged.
- People don't want to join John's team, as they know there is no future upside for them.

So, really great managers must lose their senior people, because they develop people with ability and ambition, who want to get on, and who are coveted by other managers in the business, or by outsiders. But it doesn't matter when those people go, because great managers have more, and even better, people coming through.

I've seen this happen many times - when great managers lose good people, they find (sometimes to their surprise!) that the next person coming through is even better, and is ready quickly for their chance.

Another positive effect of all this is that good people want to be in great managers' teams, as they know that they will get both development and opportunity – so great managers are never short of good people with potential wanting to work for them.

In great teams, nobody should be indispensable (including the leader!).

34) Systems are there to serve the customers and the staff, not the reverse

You'd think, with all the money being spent on IT capex, IT departments, and the related armies of consultants, that businesses would be getting real value for money, and driving value for customers, from technology.

Too often though, the reality is that nothing like value for money is achieved from these enormous spends. So, why is this happening?

One reason is that too many Boards have little or no real expertise in technology and, more relevantly, how it can be used to drive serious advantage in business. Also, if there is a CTO on the Board, he will usually just be Top Geek and not a business person or thinker.

So, the spending isn't related to the real strategy and needs of the business and its customers, as no Board member is able to connect technology expertise with business nous. The capexes are often about the latest vanity project, techie toy or trend that that the geeks want, or something being pushed by the slick sales people and consultants who infest the technology sector.

The end result is that companies (including large global blue chips) have systems that "don't talk to each other" and customers and staff get frustrated by the incompetence built into corporate IT systems, and the delays, non-delivery and outrageous costs of major projects, right through to even small requests for change.

A big part of the answer to this is for all managers to accept that they need a good in-depth knowledge of technology, if they are going to be the top managers of the future; that they need to invest in themselves by learning to use effectively all of the software at their disposal – not just how it works, but to challenge themselves to learn how it can be used more effectively to drive business advantage; and to expect that the technology teams will meet their requirements.

As well as not enough managers understanding technology, another issue is that the technology teams need to understand they only exist to meet the requirements of the people they serve, just as the business has to delight its own customers, or die.

A good way to achieve this is for the geeks to be regularly booted out of their bubbles and to be required to work and live next to the people they are serving – customers and colleagues. When they see what is really going on at the coal face and talk to real people, they will understand more easily how to generate new and better ways to do business, using their technology skills and creativity.

From the previous comments, you might think I'm not a big fan of the Geek Squad – actually, the opposite is true.

I've worked with some great technology people and installed many systems, and seen how existing technology can be bent and shaped (sometimes far from its original purpose), in order to drive tremendous business advantage.

This can apply not only to quite sophisticated systems, but also to basics such as spreadsheets and word processing.

It's amazing what can be achieved when technology people think of themselves as business people, and business people as technology people, all of them questioning how things work, looking for improvements and working together to use technology to generate business advantage.

35) The real owners of the business are the customers, closely followed by the staff – shareholders and banks come later!

There's a lot of nonsense talked in Boardrooms about focusing on shareholder value. This is reinforced by the lawyers giving directors a primary duty to look after the shareholders.

What this usually means is that Boards often spend too little time discussing how to look after the people who really do matter – the customers, then the staff. It's their "value" that really counts! Shareholders and banks tend to pay lip service to the importance of customers and staff but, when the key decisions are made, they generally focus on getting their money first before anyone else, and as quickly as possible.

If you upset the shareholders, their options are to fire you or to sell their shares. If they do that because you are focusing on looking after the customers, then you are better off elsewhere – working with shareholders who understand how great businesses are really built, over a decent period of time with investment and passion and deep caring for customers.

Upset the customers and the effect will be much worse and faster than upsetting shareholders. Customers can bring your business down and, with the viral nature of most customer sets in today's connected age, they can bring it down in double-quick time. If the owners are the people with most power in a business, then the customers are the real owners.

Similarly, upset most of the staff at your peril as, if they start to walk in numbers or lack morale or enthusiasm, your whole business is equally at peril, since they are the people who talk to and serve your customers and who your customers listen to.

By focusing first on the customers, and how to deliver value and delight to them, you can create a business with great commercial power that, as a by-product, then delivers good returns to other stakeholders such as shareholders.

The same is true of banks – pay too much attention to them and you'll neglect the real owners, the customers, who need most of the attention of every manager in the business.

Remember – there are no great businessmen, who created great businesses, whose epitaph is "he/she maximised shareholder value".

If you want to create a truly great business, keep your mind focused on the customers and the staff, and every other stakeholder will ultimately also get the rewards they want.

36) Mentors and Coaches

I used to despise the idea of mentors and coaches – seeing it a sign of weakness - until I finally found a good one, by luck more than anything.

Part of the problem was that mentoring and coaching is dressed up in so much consultancy-style speak these days that it sometimes looks and feels like a religious rite.

On top of that is the sad fact that some leaders and managers do not genuinely care enough about their team to want to invest the time to mentor and coach, or do not consider it a priority. Good signs of that for staff are when managers fix appraisal dates and then cancel. Or when managers clearly haven't done the preparation.

In large companies, the experience is also usually bound up with a great deal of process and form-filling, that tends to undermine the original good intention and frustrate everyone involved.

The reality is that mentoring and coaching is just being able to talk to some-one about the challenges and successes of the job, and to get their advice – a bit like I'm trying to talk with you today. For that to be successful, you need to find some-one who is comfortable to talk to, and who you can trust implicitly.

Given the likely stresses of your job, you definitely want some-one who will turn down the temperature in your head, not up, allowing you to think more clearly about your issues. That's really important, as it's ultimately only you who can find the solutions to your problems.

Bad coaches tend to tell you what the answer is (in their opinion). A good coach understands that his job is to help you find your own answers, in your own way and in your own time.

It can take a long while to find such a person.

37) What is Success?

A good question to ask and one that takes time to answer, and a lot of slow, deep thinking. Also a question that each person has to answer for themselves.

Today, we see images of success in business that are focused mainly around financial success, people making large amounts of money etc etc.

All of this omits the fact that luck plays a big part in a lot of this success, although the life stories of the people concerned are often dressed up to suggest that this isn't so. There are many brilliant managers and great people out there who have not made obscene amounts of money and never will.

If luck plays a big part, then that type of "success" is not going to be accessible to everyone. You may have to face up to this at some point in your career.

But, whatever different challenges life throws at us, all of us have exactly the same possibility to create the same amount of meaning and purpose in how we respond. It's how we play the game, with what we have, that shows our quality and reasons for self-respect - not the outcomes.

So, let's give everyone the chance to be successful, by redefining success as "giving everything you possibly can, and more, to hit your objectives, whilst keeping your integrity"

The truth is that real success actually lies somewhere in the struggle, not the prize. If you have done your very best, and kept your integrity, then what more is there that anyone can expect of you, or you can expect from yourself? The actual outcomes then are much less important.

If you have left nothing on the field of battle and given it your all, then you are as much a hero as anyone else.

38) Defeat and failure

If success is about doing your best in the struggle, and giving of your very best, then it's obvious that there will be times when you don't hit your formal business objectives.

The world out there calls these instances "defeat" and "failure", but you shouldn't see it that way at all. It's not, it's actually just learning.

A real failure is where some-one hasn't given it their very best shot, but even those are opportunities to learn and change, and bounce back.

My own "defeats" have felt incredibly painful, mainly because I tried so hard to hit the target objective – in that sense, they were actually "successes", although they didn't feel like it at the time! The pain itself was beneficial; once I'd calmed down and recovered and thought clearly about the lessons, I never forgot the learnings and made sure that they were fully implemented – so, that was another success out of the experience. The same is true for everyone.

Therefore "defeat" is nothing but education, the first and most important step to doing better next time, assuming you do actually think about it and learn, and make changes.

I sometimes think that the only reason I achieved some successes was that I eventually ran out of ways to fail, having thoroughly explored them all!

So, used correctly, defeat builds experience and mental toughness and creates the conditions for success.

Once "defeats" and "failures" have served their learning purpose, forget them and move on.

39) Guard your Integrity

I mentioned integrity before because I think it's a fundamental part of success, without which any financial or business achievement is ultimately hollow, or may even contain the seeds of its own destruction.

Leaders are defined by their values, and values are largely personal. But there is one value that is required of every leader and that is integrity – it is a core value. If you don't have integrity, no-one will trust you and nor should they. If leaders are not true to the values they profess, people will quickly lose confidence in their leadership.

Modern business involves many situations where your personal integrity is going to be put under great pressure or questioned – often, sadly, by colleagues or other stakeholders who have no right to expect you to compromise your reputation, by asking you to behave in ways that you will never be proud of.

In almost all cases, there's another, better way to achieve the desired objective and it isn't worth sacrificing your integrity, no matter what people want you to do. You may suffer in the short-term, but you gain more than that over a longer period. An exception may be certain situations where the people paying the price for your integrity are other people – such as your own family or friends.

Lose your integrity and you lose a big part of your reputation (see Chapter 1); and, once compromised, it will take a long time to get it back, if it even can be recovered.

Not only do you lose your reputation with other people and devalue your personal brand, you also lose self-respect and that can be more damaging internally than anything that anyone else can do to you. Your biggest and most painful critic is always yourself.

Self-respect is important to managers and leaders. When you get up in the morning and look at your face in the bathroom mirror, you need to like and respect the face looking back at you.

If you do, then that in itself is success.

40) When your leadership is questioned

One of the inevitable situations you will have to face up to is when your leadership is questioned.

This usually arises when you've had to make some problematic decisions and, because of that, it will arise at the very point when the co-operation of others is most needed, but least forthcoming. Even worse, the lack of co-operation may be unexpected or arise from people that you've previously trusted and been able to rely upon, and whose support has been essential in the past.

Worst of all, you may find that people question your personal motives and say things about you that are patently untrue, mainly behind your back.

So, it is likely to prove to be a severe personal trial.

The only answers to this are:

- To keep faith in yourself and your own decisions; <u>provided</u> you've listened and thought carefully about it, then trust yourself and follow through. A mediocre decision, well and vigorously implemented by you, usually produces a good result. The decision itself may not be the critical factor

in success. What's more, the most important person who needs to get behind your decision is you!
- To accept that, sometimes, you can't always take everyone with you. The stragglers will have to catch up later, or leave.
- To look after yourself in times of stress. When you are not getting the usual support, you need to find it elsewhere.
- To make use of your mentor as a support. This is when they can show their real value to you.
- To understand that this is also an opportunity to learn and improve. To absorb and learn from any feedback you are getting and modify your decisions, if appropriate.
- Sometimes, just to ignore the bastards who are dragging you back!

These things are sent to try us and there is no escaping them!

41) Customer Satisfaction Surveys (CSAT) – what goes wrong

When you are looking for ideas as to how to improve your business or team, the best source of good information is the very people who you are paid to delight – the customers. So, a smart thing to do is to ask them.

A whole industry has built up around how to do this and measure it, and many businesses put a great deal of effort into their CSAT surveys.

Yet the measurement systems can suffer from problems that make the results quite dangerous and delusional for the senior people who get the feedback. For example:

- There's a high volume of requested surveys, but the response rates are usually low and there's an assumption that the responders are a fair reflection of all customers; they are not – non-responders are mainly people who can't be bothered to respond or didn't want to respond. They're unlikely to be recommenders, that's for sure, and you need to hear from them.
- The surveys are just too long. People don't have the time to do page after page for you and your business and they don't want to.
- The methodology – email, internet, junior people calling – allows customers to easily

avoid responding or to rush through the survey in a way that devalues the responses, or gives nothing but scores. We've all seen those surveys that look as though they have been completed as though in a race.
- Surveys are carried out by junior or inexperienced staff, or staff from outside the business, so the answers are not probed for the truth that lies beneath.
- Staff are incorrectly involved and able to game the system to get better scores or to eliminate negative feedback (usually for bonus or other reasons). We've all had those surveys, where we are being pushed or emotionally blackmailed to give the most positive responses!
- There's no follow up, or feedback loop to show customers that they've been listened to and action taken. So customers see even less reason to participate next time as they see no benefit to themselves. "What's the point?"
- Focus is on the scores not the detailed feedback. The primary purpose of these surveys is to learn how to improve, not an artificial score. Just exactly what does it really mean if the scores have increased from 65% to 70% when there's so much risk in the measurement?

The end result is then deluded nonsense; I had that experience in a business with great "class-leading scores"; until I then asked myself why, if we were so brilliant, the customers weren't beating down the door to give us more business.

The answer was that the surveys did not properly represent what the customers were thinking; and I'd been fooling myself and missing out on the opportunity to learn and improve.

We all know of businesses like this – whose customer experience is inadequate but whose leaderships boast in public about their great CSAT scores. And we wonder "how can they possibly be getting those scores, when my experience of them is so poor?" Now you know the likely answer.

So, test your own processes against the issues I've just highlighted above and then make changes to start to get to know what your customers really think.

42) Good questions to ask customers..........the 2 questions

We made many changes to our CSAT surveys to address the issues and there were many learnings before we started to really reap the benefits.

One thing we did to make our CSAT surveys more effective was to make them very short, and to do as many as possible face to face.

Therefore, we had to make the questions as effective as possible, and we came up with the following 2 questions that worked well:

- If there's one thing we could do to improve our service to you – stop something, start something, or make some other change – what is it?
- If there's one thing that you really like about our service, what is it? (This is an excellent question to ensure you build on and reinforce what your customers actually like, as opposed to just thinking all the time about what they are unhappy with.)

These questions can be asked as part of simple regular surveys but, best of all, they could be employed in any customer situation, such as at the close of a meeting or visit by the customer. We therefore coached staff to ask the questions regularly as part of the normal interactions with customers.

The key point is that the questions are simple and can take little time to answer properly; so, response rates and the quality/depth of the answer should be high, giving credibility to the overall feedback and any repeated themes in the feedback.

This approach made it easy to act on the high quality feedback straightaway, and to tell the customers later that we'd listened and acted, and what we actually did; then to check in with them to see if they'd noticed. That way, they bought into us and never stopped wanting to give us feedback on how to get better. We proved it was a worthwhile investment of their time, unlike most of these surveys.

Most of my biggest and most valuable business lessons have come from customers who've been willing to invest like this in showing us how to do better for them. After all, who else is better placed to advise you than the people who are buying your service or product?

43) Understand your customers – you need to "get" their business and them

One of the main reasons for asking questions of customers is not just to learn about how to improve, but also to learn as much as possible about their business and themselves as people. In answering simple questions, like those in the previous chapter, customers can reveal priceless knowledge about themselves and their strategies and priorities.

It's a pretty fundamental truth that the more you know about your customers, the better your service will be and the more your customers will feel appreciated and valued when they see the investment you are making in them, to get to know them. Customers love suppliers who are genuinely interested in them and their business challenges.

That doesn't just mean asking questions – it means personal (by you) in-depth research and fingertips knowledge of all of the news about customers that is out there, as it happens, and then interacting with customers about the news. You will have to spend a lot of time on this and use the news feeds on the internet, as well as researching your customers through social media, websites and other published media, in addition to ensuring that every customer contact is fully documented and shared around your business.

The rewards for this are immense, as when one major blue-chip customer told me "you really get our business", when explaining why they gave us sole supplier status.

You also need to carry out similar levels of research on the people you are doing business with and, again, there are plenty of resources to allow you to easily connect with and learn about them – such as Google, LinkedIn, Facebook etc. A big part of business is that "people do business with people", not with companies, as shown when one customer told me we were best at Customer Experience because we made her feel "special and valued and appreciated". Note: she was not talking about her company, but herself – a subject that fascinates most people!

44) Be your own customer

An essential part of understanding your own customer's thinking is to become one yourself and see exactly what it feels like.

What's more, you'll get another viewpoint (your own) to add into the CSAT surveys sent back by customers. As an insider to the business, you'll also see more easily than your customers what can be fixed easily and quickly, and you'll see more clearly the best ideas for the future.

Yet most senior people are insulated from this reality by the corporate cocoon – they never get to see and feel in the raw the true service level that a customer of theirs experiences.

Busy execs pay fortunes to internal teams and consultants to advise them and report on what the customer experience is like, yet they could easily go and feel it for themselves.

So, sign up today with yourself, and see it for yourself.

45) Who are the customers?

Pretty much everyone that you come across in business – colleagues, bosses, staff, suppliers, customers, advisors – are to be treated as customers.

Run through the list of people you deal with and ask yourself if you are treating them all as customers.

You just don't know who anyone really is or will become in the future – for all you know, that girl in accounts could be going out with the brother of some-one who is a major influencer on your latest big pitch.

Nor you do you know if some-one who might seem unimportant now, won't become much more important to you in the future.

Treat <u>everyone</u> as a customer or potential customer and then you'll just have one mind-set that you need – that of service – and that makes your job a lot simpler.

46) All you have to do is to get them to "rub along" together

As a new manager, I wanted to solve every little problem in the team and felt personally responsible for everything. It took me a long time to realise I didn't have to do that and, by doing it, I was preventing people from learning to sort out their own problems with each other.

You see, people are people and there will inevitably be friction in a high performance and driven team environment. People will fall out with each other from time to time, over issues.

Some-one once told me that all you have to do is help people to "rub along" together. So, it's often better to tell people to sort out their own issues with other team members, only stepping in if there is real need, rather than wasting your own time on it. A high performance team will always have issues and frictions, but all they have to do is to "rub along together". It's best that they learn to do that themselves, building higher quality relationships in the process.

Of course, issues may be serious enough that you do have to step in, but that's also the time when you explain to people that their continued presence in your team may be in jeopardy, unless they can find ways to work together effectively with colleagues!

47) The importance of leaders setting an example

One of the first things that any leader does is to set an example. And the example has to be strong enough to command people's respect and to make them want to follow and imitate.

A lot of managers don't understand how critical this is – but people will only truly follow those who they respect, and that respect must be earned.

As soon as some people become managers, they start to take advantage of their power and trust – e.g. by coming in later and taking time off for golf, or abusing the expenses system (in several cases buying lingerie for their wives, at least I assumed it was their wives, on the company), or using the company builder to do free work on their homes. Often they are just reflecting the values that they have seen in the people above them. Sometimes, it's just because they want to show off their power – "I do it because I can now, and want everyone to see it."

Their people see these behaviours and that affects how they behave and the way they view the business and their manager. It then spreads as people talk about the leader behind his back - there are very few real secrets in business.

If leaders want to make fools of themselves in front of the staff and erode any moral authority they have, they should just carry on behaving like this.

And they shouldn't expect their staff to behave any better than they are, or be surprised when they don't.

But, if managers want to be successful through building and empowering a great team, a good starting point is the example they set for others – let's therefore set one that we will always be proud of, for all time, and that others who come after us will be inspired by!

You choose.

48) Learning - what did you learn today?

Great businesses are experimenters (where staff are encouraged to propose and try out new ideas, and for it to be OK if new ideas don't work).

Experimenting businesses are learning business, if the experiments are handled correctly. Most experiments don't come right the first time; success often comes only after many setbacks and failures.

Learning and experimenting business are continually improving businesses, the ones with the best chances of long-term success.

But, in the hurly-burly of daily business, it's hard to create this experimenting and learning mentality.

One way which I've found powerful is to keep on asking the question "what did we learn today (and what is going to change as a result)?" This question can be used in different situations, but it demands that the team are always looking to try out new ways to get better, as a business or themselves.

The question can be adapted to a situation where something has gone wrong, and the team need to avoid the knee-jerk reaction of focusing on 1) Who is to blame and 2) How do we get out of this with the least possible cost or embarrassment. Problems and issues are great opportunities, as the painful lessons are never forgotten; they can also be the best opportunities to show customers by your reaction that you are different, special, unique.

The question is also very useful in situations where things have gone well. Inviting your team to review what they learned from success will reinforce the reasons for success, and be the surest way to repeating it or building on it. Also, there is nothing like success to generate a wave of confidence in a team; so, thinking and talking about the learnings from success will, in itself, increase the chances of more to come, as people are encouraged to keep on experimenting and learning and changing.

The learning mentality in a business has to visibly apply to everyone, and every day. I've seen various ways to achieve this such as messages on office walls saying: "what have you learnt today, and how will this change things to make us stronger? Don't go home until you can answer this question". Find your own ways.

However you do it, encouraging a learning and experimenting mentality throughout a business is just another facet of the drive to create the "power of the many" in a business – getting as many people as possible on board with the strategy and giving their all to achieve it, because they know they can propose or try new things, make a difference and be appreciated for sticking their necks out.

49) Good people are all around you

Pretty much most of the capability that you need to build a great business or team is likely (but not certain) to be already there in your team, if you can but see it.

I think that many companies are getting out of their people, overall, nothing like the capability and potential that lies hidden within.

The truth is that most people are frustrated with their jobs and, at the heart of much of the frustration, lies the fact that their employers are using very little of the latent capability in the whole staff, and are not giving many of their people the chance to stretch and grow, and play a bigger role.

Most people want to be stretched and developed, and to achieve their potential, and to find value and meaning in what they are spending much of their waking hours working at – their jobs.

Your role as a manager is to help them to discover their ability, and then to support them in bringing it to life.

And then be amazed by the results!

50) Take your team away (and what to do)

If you are going to build a high performance business, you need to build a high performance team; to do this, I don't believe you need to socialise a lot with your team, but you do need regular quality time with them outside of the working environment.

I'm not talking about going to the pub after work, although that may be useful, but rather taking the team away for at least a day and an overnight stay, if you can – preferably somewhere that has poor mobile reception and difficulty in getting e-mails!

You need to get people well away from the workplace and into an environment where they can get some serious uninterrupted time together, in order to build better quality relationships than are achievable just in the workplace.

What should you do? I've found 2 approaches that have worked well.

Firstly, using a facilitator to organise a series of structured activities. That worked well when the team was first "forming" and the ice needed to be broken in terms of willingness to share more openly. An essential part of the success of this approach was finding the right facilitator; there are many people who are in this business but few who have the right practical mind-set and understanding of business.

A second approach was to take the team on a long walk when we circulated in pairs discussing pre-agreed topics such as "How are you feeling about the business at the moment", or "what do you think I or the team could do better, and where do you think we are doing well". All of this was then developed in open forum over dinner, and at breakfast the next day. This second approach worked well when the team was more established and confident enough with each other.

Both approaches were based around a stay in a hotel.

Both approaches also yielded significant steps forward in building a high performance team that could generate high performance in the business.

They were well worth the investment in time and cost.

51) Getting time alone; sharpening your axe; investing in yourself

I've talked a lot in this book about investing in people, including taking the team away from the office, but it's also essential that you invest directly in yourself, and do this regularly.

This isn't just about having a mentor/coach, although that can be incredibly valuable; bluntly, you need to get some regular quality time alone where you do nothing connected with your business, and where you aren't necessarily "doing" anything at all.

Today's business environment conspires against managers taking time out and we end up with managers who are working all the hours possible and more. They believe themselves to be giving it everything they've got, but the reality is that they are not as effective as they could be.

Some key things that are important for busy managers include:

- You must take every last day of your holiday entitlement and let your staff know that emails and calls are for really important stuff only, so you switch off; you should also insist that your staff do the same and ban roll-over of holidays into the next year.

> These holidays are there for a reason – you all need a break to stay fresh.
- If you have a family, you need time set aside for them to take your mind off work, as well as achieving balance in your life.
- You also need regular time each week which is your time and no-one else's. That may involve sport or meeting friends – whatever works for you.
- Within work, you need to reserve time when your door is shut and e-mails/phone calls are deferred.

Not all of the above ideas may work for you, and you may have different ideas – but the underlying principles apply to everyone. If you don't take regular time out to sharpen your axe, your axe will get blunt and your effectiveness will decrease.

There is no escape from this. No-one is superhuman and the mind and body need looking after, if you are going to complete the marathon that most business success requires.

People who are working excessive hours over a very long period, without any break, ultimately are not Being the Best for themselves, their families or their businesses.

52) Everyone in your business or team can have a huge influence on success

Most companies pay lip service to the importance of every member of staff; they have fancy policies talking about their culture, they win Investors in People and other types of award etc etc.

Yet they display their true values by how they actually treat different classes of people in their business; it's generally the directors who are being given obscene salaries, enormous bonuses, whopping pay-offs (sometimes to buy their silence and in return for failure) and fancy benefits and offices – being treated as though they are irreplaceable; while the people on the front line are being told that there's no or little pay increase and certainly no bonus, and they are treated in every way as though they are eminently replaceable. Yet many of them aren't, as no company can afford to lose good people at any level, particularly who work directly with customers.

The truth is that, although the differentials on reward structures often don't fairly reflect this, everyone is important and everyone can influence the small difference that exists between success and failure in business.

At one of the businesses I worked in, we had some receptionists and one of them handled visitors to Head Office. She smiled at visitors, made them tea and did everything possible to make them feel welcome. Over the years, I lost count of the number of my visitors who made unsolicited comments about how good she was and how much they enjoyed coming to see us as a result.

It wasn't just about "manning a reception" in an age when many companies don't consider reception to be important, having just a phone there.

It was actually all about making visitors feel welcome (Customer Experience) and everyone in a business can critically influence this. It's amazing what customers notice, particularly when they don't get it elsewhere.

It may be impossible financially to hand out pay increases to everyone who deserves one. But behaviour like this has to be publicly celebrated and rewarded if you are going to spread it everywhere round your team and business, as you need to do if you want success.

People can feel good about themselves and their work, without it always having to involve money.

53) Importance of Persistence/Enduring and how

There's no doubt that most success comes through persistent and unremitting effort over a long period of time, and often the most outstanding success comes after people just refuse to quit on their objectives.

So, endurance (sticking it out) or persistence (keeping on trying) are clearly essentials in the toolkits of managers. What's less clear is how to endure, or how to persist.

There's plenty of advice out there on how to do this – meditate, find a mentor, write down your objectives and focus on them every day, breathing exercises, sport etc etc. All of these may have some value.

But the fundamental truth is that endurance is one of those qualities that cannot be taught in advance but only learnt by doing it. The mental fortitude that underpins people who endure comes from within, and it is created and nourished largely by <u>repeated acts of endurance</u>. Each person can only find the capacity to endure inside themselves – they only learn, during those periods of pain and intense pressure, how they themselves can stand it and carry on, in their own way.

Therefore, you only learn to endure by actually enduring – doing it.

So, go out and starting digging your heels in and refusing to quit! And when you get knocked down or defeated, get up again and keep going, or start again!

And do it with high levels of enthusiasm, passion and commitment to your cause – enduring is meant to be positive and energising. Perseverance and endurance are not about just lasting the distance; they are about doing it in a way that means you will have left absolutely nothing on the field of play, when they finally carry you off, and you'll be proud of how you played the game to the end!

54) Climbing a mountain

Many business tasks look like climbing a mountain; it can be impossible to see how the task will be completed, before you begin.

Or it may even appear that you and your team are not capable of reaching the summit.

The truth is that many teams are not capable of reaching the summit before they start climbing the mountain, but they get fit along the way. The process of climbing makes them good enough to get to the top.

I've met many so-called "talented" people who weren't seen as talented when they started out; they just became talented along the way, thanks to the sacrifices they were prepared to make to gain the skills they needed.

So, unless something is truly impossible, the best thing that you and your team can do, when confronted with something that appears hard is (after some preliminary thought) to get started, to get climbing; and, once you've started, keep going.

55) Numbers/forecasting and action

When you're climbing the mountain, there are plenty of things that can get in the way of the most important thing - you keeping going. And one of the most common of these is the amount of time spent on "the numbers."

There's no shortage of people connected with business - the shareholders, analysts, bankers, your boss, the CFO etc. - whose lives can seem to revolve wholly around the results and forecasts coming out of your business or team.

These well-intentioned people can be the bane of your life, as you struggle to drive business improvement or transformation, particularly if things aren't going so well. They want to feel that they too are "adding value" or "doing something about it" and they often think they can achieve this by demanding endless re-forecasts and detailed analyses. Part of the reason for this may be to respond to the needs of the audiences they themselves report in to.

Now, don't get me wrong; having high quality plans, information and detail in respect of your business is essential to understanding where you've got to and what you need to do next. But, once you have that, what's required is 100% focus on continuous vigorous action in pursuit of your objectives. Only that will make things better.

I can tell you from experience that you will never improve the numbers by staring at them, or continually reforecasting, or producing endless different analyses. Businesses are not contained in spreadsheets; they're about products and services, and customers and staff – and it's continuous action here that's needed to generate improvement.

And, since you're a professional manager, not a clairvoyant, your ability to forecast the future is actually very limited – most plans are out of sync with reality from the moment they are published. You can't really see that far into the future and long-term forecasting is usually just guesswork that will be proved wrong by events.

So, the most important thing is that you keep 100% focused on doing the right things, in sufficient quantity and vigorously enough. Then, the numbers will have the best chance to eventually "take care of themselves."

56) Listening

One of the hardest things I've found as a manager is to be a good listener. When you're completely obsessed with your own ideas and objectives, it's hard to take a genuine interest in what is on the minds of others, which can sometimes seem unimportant or less relevant to the overall business strategy. This must still be one of my several weak areas, despite years of effort!

Yet nearly all business success comes either through others or with the co-operation and active support of others; and that support is more readily given when people believe you are willing to listen to their concerns.

What's more, if they are the ones who are delivering your strategy on the front line, then their concerns and worries have got to be right at the top of your agenda, because that's what is on their minds.

There's plenty of amusing books on different techniques on how to be a good listener, the most useful one I've found it is to let people talk first – i.e. to listen first.

More than the techniques, I think good listening fundamentally comes down to one key factor - just what is the level of your genuine interest in your people? If you really do care about them and their concerns more than your own, then you're likely to be a good listener, as you're already interested.

Of course, if you don't care that much about your people, then perhaps you shouldn't be in management in the first place.

57) Courage/bravery/risk

If you are going to be a proper manager, there will be times when you have to do things that are brave, as they involve risk.

It may be a decision to dismiss a longstanding or apparently important employee; or to tell your boss that he's got it wrong; or, as I've done on a number of occasions, a decision that effectively bets the company and therefore risks everyone's livelihood. Or to say no to your bankers, or shareholders – I've done the former and should have done a lot more of the latter!

How do you deal with these situations?

The first thing to remember is that there are no brave actions unless you're feeling scared, sometimes really scared – we all know that bad feeling in the pit of the stomach that tells you this one could go badly wrong and you are the one who they will all blame. So remind yourself that everyone who takes a brave decision feels exactly as you do – you are not alone. And consider how the fear can be used effectively to generate a better decision and a more powerful and dynamic implementation.

Once you understand that these feelings are normal and you're in good company, you then just need to get a bit of perspective on this:

firstly, whatever decision you take, in a hundred years' time, no-one will care about it – so any shame or embarrassment, if you get it wrong, is only temporary and people will care a lot less than you think after a short while; secondly, get it into your head, unlike many other managers, that doing nothing is not available as a cop-out; that too is a decision with risk that you are making, and for which you can be blamed. So, there is no escape – this is why you are paid to be a manager; now is when you earn your pay.

In terms of taking the decision, take as much useful time as you can to think it through. That doesn't mean forever – all decisions need to be taken or the impact of no decision starts to hurt (unless "no decision" is the decision); what it does mean is that you think it through as carefully as you can; that's being responsible.

Then, try to get to a position where you can convince yourself that there is really only one decision/action that you can take. In pretty much all of my toughest decisions that people later thought were brave, I'd already convinced myself that there was only one viable alternative that I'd want to live with. So, questions of bravery or risk became irrelevant; I thought I could do nothing else and just needed to get on with it!

For the really troubling decisions, it's worthwhile talking it through with an experienced person who you can trust to give you an impartial view; generally, this should be some-one who is not at the coal-face with you and who is therefore able to stand back from the situation and look at it in a different and unemotional way. That person is not, however, a substitute decision-maker; the decisions are yours and yours alone.

Once you've gone through all of that, the only thing left is to be brave and JFDI – Just Flaming Do It!

Then, if you're an effective manager and you've thought it through, you'll deal with the consequences, including the unexpected ones, as they arise. Very few decisions pan out in the way expected, so management readiness for action after the event is crucial.

58) Waiting/Patience

"If you can wait and not be tired by waiting" – from Rudyard Kipling's poem "If".

Waiting is not something that managers like to do much of in today's world; too much of our time is spent rushing because we believe we are time-poor; rushing from one meeting to another; rushing to meet a deadline; rushing to finish a report; rushing home to get that precious hour with the wife or kids.

A lot of the rushing is driven by the idea that things are needed now; in many cases, they aren't but, if it's your boss or your customers who are saying this then it's their time that you have to run by; so, quite a lot of the rushing will always be impossible for you to control in today's world.

But some of it is under our control and I want to particularly point out the rushing we do to answer questions or to solve problems. It's a feature of modern managers that many of them believe that all problems need to be solved and quickly. Actually, that isn't true of everything.

As an action-oriented manager who, if there was an itch always wanted to go and scratch it, I took far too long to learn that some problems look better (or a solution presents itself) if you wait; and some problems just solve themselves or vanish in some other way.

So, if you have a problem, before you start to invest your time in it, ask yourself whether, at this time, you need do anything at all. Or whether waiting is an option that might make a real difference and deliver a better answer, and a better use of your time.

Another important feature of waiting is that sometimes you just have to – you cannot always force things to happen when you want them to. A good illustration of this is the fact that expectations about results and the impact of management activity are often much too optimistic; it usually takes longer than people wish for the benefits to come through, even though everyone may be trying their best.

Provided you are doing all of the right things, vigorously and intensely, then you sometimes just have to trust that eventually "the numbers will take care of themselves". Keeping on plugging away as hard as you can, and not giving up, is another form of waiting that great managers and leaders understand.

59) Blame is pointless (so don't point!)

An enormous amount of management activity is concerned with blame:

- Avoiding it
- Deciding or ensuring that no-one is blamed
- Pointing the finger of blame at others.

You need to avoid being involved in any of this and concentrate on the business and your team.

If something goes wrong, it's much more important to focus on putting it right and making the changes so that the business seizes the great opportunity to learn and improve, and the situation doesn't repeat.

You also have to remember that the blame game never achieves anything useful or positive in business; it makes everyone feels nervous and sometimes results in the wrong people being held to account. It also creates an atmosphere where people feel uncomfortable about owning up and taking responsibility for issues, so even more opportunities to learn and improve are lost.

Clearly, if people can't do their jobs, then that has to be addressed by coaching or changes in staff. But, insofar as possible, it's best to keep blame right out of business and management.

60) Saying sorry – showing vulnerability

Previous chapters discussed how "thanks" and "well done" are important phrases to use regularly and in as public a way as possible.

"Sorry"," I got it wrong", are also important things to say for managers, who want to build a long-term dynamic relationship with their teams.

This is a really tough call for many managers to take on board as the prevailing concept of leadership is one where leaders never make mistakes and, if they do, they are vilified for it. The possibility of lawsuits arising from any kind of mistake is also a factor that managers must now take into account.

That leads to behaviours which do no good – such as an unwillingness to admit fault, pointing of fingers in other directions and less ability to do the most important thing - which is to learn from setbacks and move on, growing stronger and better as a result. What's more, managers who cannot show vulnerability encourage the same sorts of behaviours in their teams, with further loss of opportunity to grow and to learn.

Consider the benefits of owning up to and taking responsibility for mistakes:

- It demonstrates great strength of character by the leader to the team. Everyone knows how tough it is to "take the blame".
- It takes the pressure of others who are responsible, and those who may be even more responsible than you, and allows a better quality and faster discussion to fix the problem and to learn from it.
- It avoids all of the wasted time and effort that goes on in businesses trying to work out who to blame; so the learnings can be grasped more quickly.
- Teams know what the truth is and, when leaders take responsibility and show vulnerability, the most likely response is loyalty and support, particularly when it's clear that the leader is deliberately taking the flak. The payback here for leaders is many times the investment.

An earlier chapter discussed how real leaders should be the last to take the credit. They should also be the first to take responsibility and, if necessary, the blame – to be the scapegoat.

Therefore, when things have gone wrong, aim to be the first to step forward, to start the process of putting it right.

61) Loneliness – you are on your own

A lot of this book has been about the interaction of managers and leaders with other people, and the tremendous strength and power that can be derived from this.

However, there will be times when you realise that one of the consequences of leadership is that, occasionally, you are on your own.

It may be at a time when your leadership is questioned or undermined. It may be when an important decision has to be taken and only you can take that decision alone. It may be when you are not getting the support you expect and deserve, or are misunderstood, as you battle with business issues. Or even when disloyalty and unprofessional behaviour from other people, who you have trusted, saps away at your motivation and will to succeed.

Whatever and whenever it is, you will realise that one of the essential parts of being a leader or manager is loneliness. You are truly alone – like other managers who have been there, and know how you are feeling. At these times, there's often little help for you as shareholders, team, colleagues, family melt away from you, or even undermine your morale and ability to lead and manage. This is when you earn your money and show your class - because you have the ability and the personality, and the sheer grit and the will, to stand alone, to stay firm and keep going.

Some thoughts for this time:

- Being alone may actually be enough – as one manager trying his best to do the right things for the business and the team, is actually a majority! Have faith in yourself.
- Since these times are going to happen, you need to prepare for them. It's crucial that you work over the years to build up your physical, mental and spiritual health, so you are ready for the times of trial when it is indeed only you and there is no help from anywhere.
- Maintaining your authentic behaviours (the authenticity we discussed before) is also essential to coming through this "dark night" in the best possible way. Irrespective of the pressure, continue to be that motivated, committed, professional, people-oriented manager who is the real you. It's at these times of pressure when all managers' real personalities show through and some fail the test. If you can just hang on in and keep showing consistency and authenticity of behaviour, and the strength of character that is the real you, then the impact on those around who are watching your trial

will be profound and lasting and positive. You will earn both respect and loyalty.
- Self-respect is also key to getting through; so try hard not to compromise your integrity or personal values, no matter how others are behaving.
- Try to be kinder and more forgiving of those who may not be giving the support you expect, or who are compromising their values. People are fallible and, under extreme pressure can get bent out of shape and do things that they are later embarrassed by, or even ashamed of. It doesn't make them bad people or people you can't work well with in the future. Be more forgiving, particularly when you consider how you've also let people down and that you'd also like to be forgiven for your failings.
- Try also to be kinder and more forgiving to yourself during this time. While you are giving everything (and more) to show all of these authentic leadership qualities under intense pressure, you're unlikely to be perfect. But you don't have to be perfect – you just have to be good enough; so, keep going until the game is over!

Lastly keep your sense of humour. These times don't last forever and, as well as learning from them, you'll should try to joke about them in the future!

62) Pride

We've been discussing a lot of things which are effectively about pride in yourself and the example you set.

Clearly, that's crucial, but equally important is that you insist on those standards and pride from everyone in your team or business. That means not just pride in the work, but pride in everything that happens at all times - for example:

- Pride in appearance. Everyone should always look as smart and professional as possible, appropriate to their role in business.
- Dress down days, which are increasingly popular, do not mean that people can come in unwashed or unshaved, or looking like muggers or tramps or tarts!
- Pride in environment; that means tidy desks and working environments. More importantly, everyone having an attitude of responsibility for the whole work environment, not just their bit, by fixing or reporting things as they spot them.

You see, pride is not something that can be applied selectively to parts of what you and your team do; it has to apply to everything or nothing. It's a mind-set that infects a business for good or, if absent, for ill.

If you don't get this right and insist on it being universal, this is what can happen:

- People who do matter to your business notice and judge you accordingly – customers, shareholders, interview candidates, your boss, the banks etc.
- The example we are using - low standards of appearance or environment – is just a starting point for a lack of pride; that then can <u>infect</u> and drag down standards elsewhere – i.e. in the quality of work or customer service.
- The attitude of just not being bothered then becomes widespread through the business and, like weeds in a garden, can be incredibly hard to root out.

I know that my view on this won't be popular everywhere, or will be seen as unrealistic; the trend in many business is for a slackening in all-round standards of corporate behaviour.

Nonetheless, I think that pride in everything is a fundamental characteristic of a successful leader, team or business. That pride needs to be evident in everything and everywhere, and at all times – no exceptions!

63) Just do it!

Some of the content of this book may have been new or even motivating to you; other parts you will already know, or may have read elsewhere.

Yet, unless you are the world's greatest manager, much of what you've read and been enthusiastic about isn't going to get done, and isn't done at all in most UK businesses. Why?

- Cost pressures (but think of the extra long-term profits from delighted customers, who are then recommenders).
- Short term profit is too important, shareholder value is paramount (but ask yourself who really owns the company, and who should be looked after first? The customers! Other stakeholder returns follow from that).
- Just too busy - meetings, reports, away days, courses. (Too busy to do what we should be doing).
- I'll look a fool if this doesn't work (we need to stop that stopping us; many successful people looked foolish to the rest of us, when they started down their track).
- Politics: sticking your head above the parapet, and doing something different, won't do you any good (but never taking any risks will miss out on your true capability).

- My boss won't support this (that's because he isn't doing it either and he needs to change and stop holding you back from helping him and the business).
- When we do it, we try to do too much at once (so, change bit by bit; one small change each week, vigorously implemented and followed through, adds up to enormous changes over the course of a year).

Stop making the excuses and just get on and start doing it! Make the changes.

Or write to me and tell me what your excuse is.

Then this will be just the latest management book you've read, where you took away some really good stuff and then did nothing about it – wasting your time in reading yet another book, and my time in writing it!

Afterword

So, here we are at the end. Thank you for investing your time to get this far.

There'll be ideas in this book that you probably haven't agreed with and, hopefully, some things that really stood out and made you think slowly, deeply and practically, on your own, about the challenges and opportunities in your own work, and what you need to change. I'd like to think that you will want to come back to it again and again, to help you discover some new truth that works for you.

If it's done at least that much good, then it will have been worth the effort on my part. And you can make me feel it's been worthwhile by giving me feedback on how to improve future editions – by posting a review on Amazon or by dropping me a line at mark@bethebestbusiness.co.

Lastly, I hope that you'll also recommend the book to others, whose thinking it can stimulate, to help them improve. By doing that you'll be my partner in spreading any value around to a wider audience.

Thanks and good luck!

Mark Bates

Printed in Great Britain
by Amazon.co.uk, Ltd.,
Marston Gate.